LEARNING WORKS PARENTS & PRESCHOOLERS SERIES

CLASSIFYING CAT

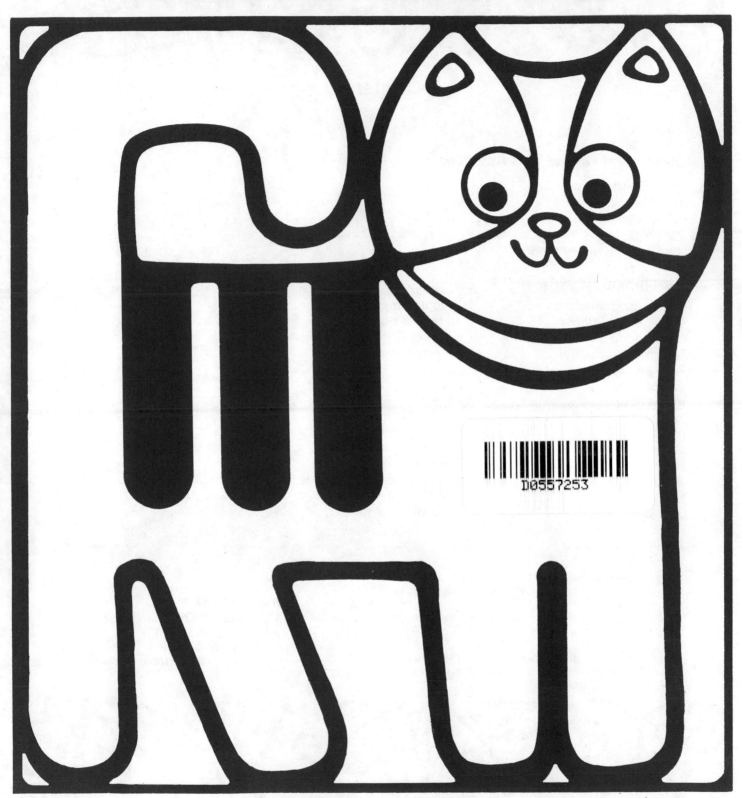

WRITTEN BY BETTY ISAAK
ILLUSTRATED BY BEV ARMSTRONG

Contents

Copyright © 1982
THE LEARNING WORKS, INC.
Santa Barbara, CA 93111
All rights reserved.
Printed in the United States of America.

Introduction

Classifying Cat has been written to help you help your child increase his or her skill at classifying. It is divided into two main sections. The first section contains brief descriptions of easy-to-play games and easy-to-do activities you and your child can enjoy together using common materials you probably have around the house.

The second section contains activity sheets for your child. On each sheet are simple instructions you can read to your child. In the upper left-hand corner are the categories the child is asked to consider in classifying the objects pictured on the page. These activities will involve your child in a variety of valuable educational experiences, including

- naming and identifying
- matching and pairing
- comparing and classifying
- drawing and coloring
- cutting and pasting

Classifying is the process of arranging things in groups or categories on the basis of shared characteristics. Classifying enables us to see relationships and to describe similarities and differences. It is an important skill for beginning readers because, to read, they must be able to recognize the shared characteristics of words and to understand their similarities and differences. As they learn to read and write, they must hear subtle differences in sound, learn degrees of meaning, and use words correctly according to their grammatical classifications. Classifying is also a first step toward logical thinking and reasoning.

In doing these activities with your child, first, have him or her name each of the pictured objects. Second, talk about the categories into which these objects are to be classified. To see if your child understands these categories, have him or her name one member of each category or choose from among the pictured objects one member for each category. Third, read and explain the activity instructions to your child and have him or her classify one or two of the objects and color, mark, or paste them as directed. Fourth, when you are certain that your child understands the categories and knows how the activity should be done, allow him or her to continue in the same manner until he or she has finished the page. Correct the page together for immediate feedback.

Classifying is a natural process, but one that can be improved with practice. This book is designed to help you give your child that all-important practice.

Classifying Games and Activities

In the Bedroom

Toy Toss (classifying by type)
Provide individual bags or boxes into which your child can sort his or her toys according to type (*examples:* balls, cars, dolls, games, stuffed animals).

Dresser Messer (classifying by type)
Tape pictures of different types of clothing on the drawers of your child's chest of drawers (*examples:* a shirt on one drawer and socks on another). Have your child clean out the drawers and sort the clothes back into them according to the picture signs. This can be taken a step further by having children subclassify items. For example, shirts can be classified as T-shirts, undershirts, and the like, or can be classified by the season in which they are worn.

Hangup Hits (classifying by type)
Put different colors of tape at intervals on the bar in your child's closet. Make a picture chart showing which type of clothing belongs with each color of tape. Post the chart on the closet door to help your child keep his or her closet in order.

In the Laundry Room

Towel Type (classifying by type, color, or pattern)
Have your child sort towels after they have been washed. Possible categories for sorting could be type (bath, dish, or hand), color, or pattern.

Sock Sort (classifying by color, pattern, or size)
Have your child help sort and pair socks after washing. Then have him or her sort matched pairs into size piles for each family member.

Which Wash (classifying by type)
Have your child help sort clothing into color or fabric categories for washing. Then have him or her sort washed and dried items into piles for distribution to different family members.

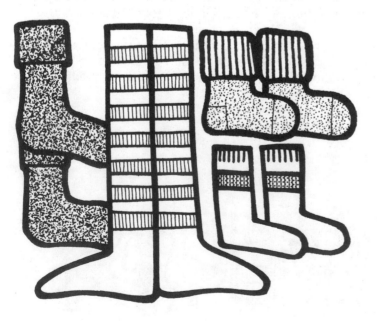

Classifying Games and Activities

In the Kitchen

Can Categories (classifying by type)
Have your child sort and classify different types of canned food in the cupboard (*examples:* fruits, soups, vegetables).

Mean Bean (classifying by type)
Purchase several small bags of different types of dried beans. Pour all of the beans into a large plastic container with a lid. Have your child sort the beans according to type.

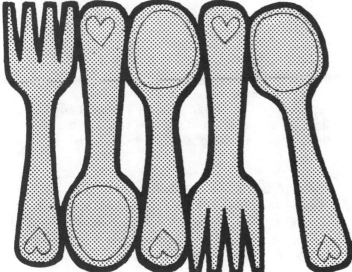

Plate Mate (classifying by size)
Have your child sort dishes that have been washed and dried into the cupboard by type or size.

Fork Finder (classifying by type)
Let your child help you clean cupboards or drawers. Encourage him or her to be a super silverware sorter by properly grouping forks, spoons, and knives.

Silly Cereal (classifying by shape or color)
Purchase cereal that contains pieces of several different colors or shapes. Have your child sort pieces of cereal into shape or color categories.

Tasty Treats (classifying by taste and smell)
Get out various foods from the pantry. Have your child taste and smell each one. Then let him or her sort them into taste categories (*examples:* sweet, sour, salty, or bitter) or into the simpler categories of *like* and *dislike*.

Classifying Games and Activities

In the Kitchen

Sort a Store (classifying by type)

Save various empty containers from foods and other products used in the home. Help your child use these containers to set up a play store. Have your child sort them by category and arrange them for display in related stacks or rows.

Munchy Match (classifying by type)

Help your child cut out pictures of assorted fruits and vegetables and sort them by category into either an empty fruit can or an empty vegetable can.

Outdoors

Rocky Road (classifying by size, shape, or color)

Help your child make a collection of small rocks. Encourage him or her to classify them according to size, shape, and color. Have your child create his or her own categories, as rocks are a favorite of children.

Sound Seeker (classifying sounds)

Take a listening walk with your child. Make a list of the sounds you hear. When you return home, classify these sounds by source. Were they made by people, animals, or vehicles?

Outdoor Order (classifying into living and nonliving categories)

Take a nature walk with your child. Collect interesting objects along the way. When you return home, classify these objects according to whether they are (or were) living or nonliving.

Classifying Games and Activities

Here, There, and Anywhere

Color Cups (classifying by color)

Using crayons or marking pens, write a different color name on each of six paper cups. Write each name in the color it names. For example, write the word *red* with a red crayon or marking pen. Have your child sort pieces of old and broken crayons into these cups according to color.

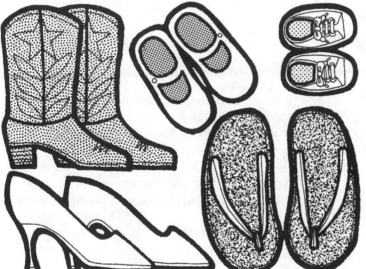

Book Nook (classifying by color, size, or type)

Help your child sort his or her books using one or more of the following criteria: cover color, size, type of story, whether read or not read.

Shoe Scramble (classifying by size or type)

Have all family members remove their shoes and put them in a pile. Scramble them. Then have everyone take a turn at matching the pairs correctly and returning them to their owners. Another variation is classifying by buckle or tie shoes, play or dress shoes.

Money Mixup (classifying by type)

Collect all the change you can. Have your child sort the coins into piles or stacks according to type (*examples:* pennies, nickels, dimes, quarters).

Tool Pool (classifying by purpose)

Help your child sort household tools by type or purpose. Use the following categories: tools that are used to pound; tools that help you put in screws; tools that cut things; tools that hold things together or in place.

Classifying Games and Activities

Here, There, and Anywhere

Fur, Feathers, or Scales (classifying by type)
Help your child cut out pictures of mammals, birds, and reptiles. Then have him or her sort these pictures according to the animals' body coverings—fur, feathers, or scales.

Funny Feeling (classifying by texture)
Cut small pieces of fabric of different textures. Have your child sort these pieces according to the way they feel, whether smooth or rough, soft or hard, limp or stiff.

Category Calls (classifying by type)
Name a category, such as *Things that are red* or *Things that are round.* Then challenge your child to discover how many items belonging to that category he or she can see and/or name.

Familiar Food (classifying by type)
Help your child cut out magazine pictures of different types of food. Then have your child sort the pictures to indicate foods that he or she has tasted or not tasted before.

Face Finder (classifying by facial expression)
Help your child cut out pictures of people's faces. Then have him or her sort the pictures according to the feelings or emotions they reflect (*examples:* happiness or anger, joy, sadness or sorrow).

Sounds and Smells

Look at the picture on the left. Is it something you **hear** or something you **smell**? If it makes a sound you **hear**, draw a circle around the girl who is listening. If it has a scent you **smell**, draw a circle around the boy who is smelling.

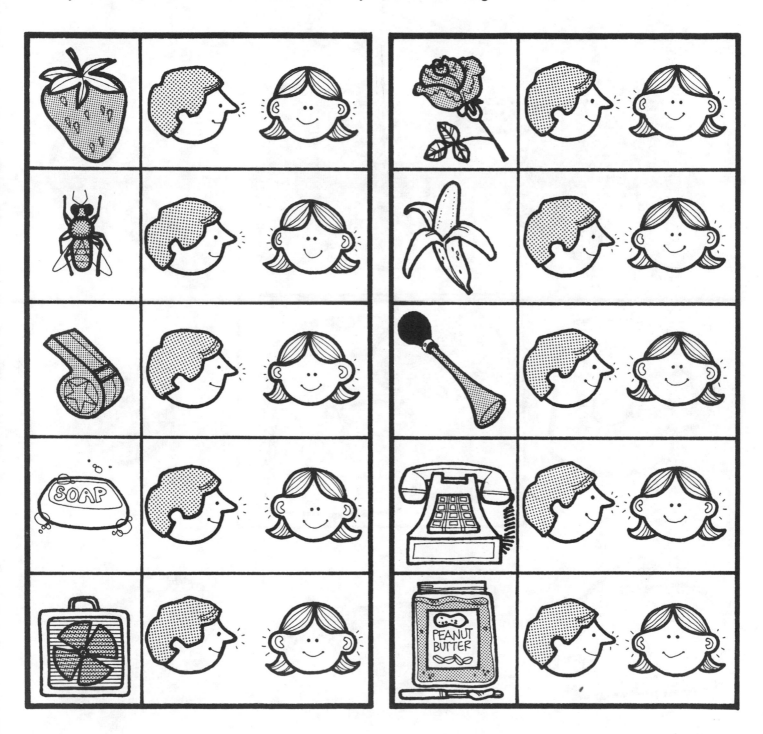

Pebbles and Pillows

Draw a line from each picture to the pebble if the object feels **hard** or to the pillow if the object feels **soft**.

Pebble

Pillow

Fire and Ice

Look at the objects pictured below. If the object is normally **hot**, color it red. If the object is normally **cold**, color it blue.

To Eat or Not to Eat

Color the yummy face beside each object that is something you **eat.** Color the yucky face beside each object that is something you **do not eat.**

Pick Six

Find and color the six foods that are vegetables.

Travel Time

Draw a circle around each of the pictured means of transportation that almost always travels on land.

In the Soup

Draw a circle around each **letter**.

Zoo's Who

Cut out the pictures of the animals below. Paste each animal's picture in the house if
it is a pet or in the cage if it is a **wild** or **zoo animal**.

In the Doghouse

Draw a green circle around all of the pictured objects that are **living**. Draw a line from all of the pictured objects that are **nonliving** to the doghouse.

Land, Water, or Air

Draw a line from each animal to the place it likes to be most of the time.

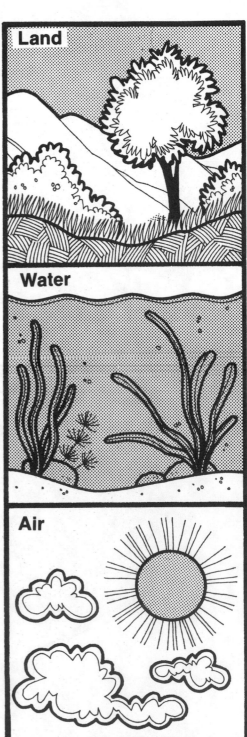

Land

Water

Air

Farm Friends

Draw a circle around each animal that belongs on a farm.

Shape Up

Color all **circles** purple; color all **squares** green; color all **triangles** blue; and color all **rectangles** orange.

◯ = purple
▢ = green
△ = blue
▭ = orange

Use the code to color the shapes.

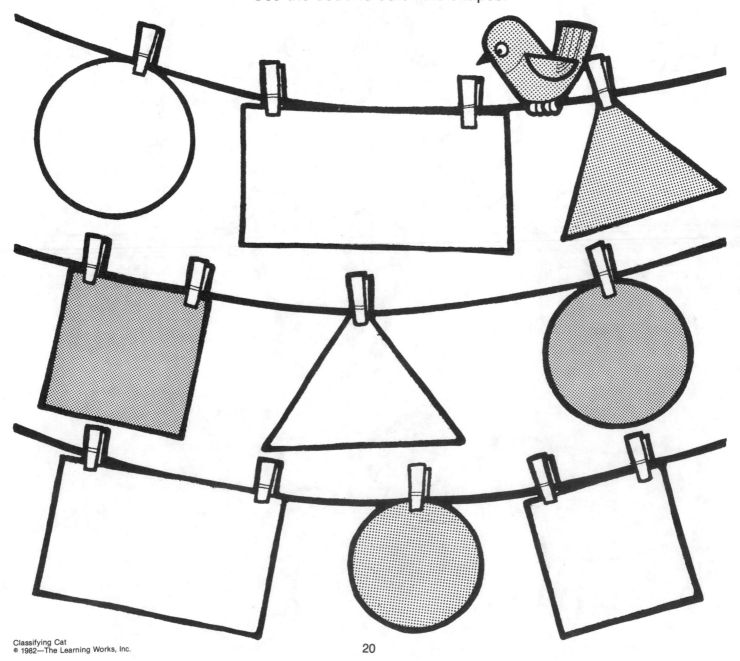

Leaves or Legs

Cut out the pictures at the bottom of the page. Identify each picture and paste it on the tree if it is a **plant** or on the elephant if it is an **animal.**

Size Wise

Color red the objects that are usually **large** and color blue the objects that are usually **small.**

This is to certify that

_____

(name of child)

is a

Clever Classifier

_____

(signature of parent)

_____

(date)

NOTES